Dear "S":
    I hope you enjoy this *rare* book *now*
I found. It is extremely funny in places
— & I trust it will take away some of
your "gloom & doom"
    Love from "D" — Christmas 2009.

PUNCH in the Air

"*But they are switched off—look!*"

PUNCH
IN THE AIR

A cartoon history of flying

Edited by David Langdon

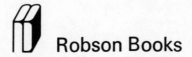
Robson Books

FIRST PUBLISHED IN GREAT BRITAIN IN 1983 BY
ROBSON BOOKS LTD., BOLSOVER HOUSE,
5-6 CLIPSTONE STREET, LONDON W1P 7EB.
COPYRIGHT © 1983 PUNCH PUBLICATIONS LTD.

British Library Cataloguing in Publication Data

Punch in the air.
1. Aeronautics–Caricatures and cartoons
741.5'0942   NC1478

ISBN 0-86051-251-7

Printed in Hungary

Introduction

Ever since man first climbed down from his tree, found the ground not all that it was cracked up to be, and gazed longingly aloft into the far cerulean welkin and its winging wildlife, he has been obsessed by a great dream.

One day, somehow, he would overcome the extraordinary difficulties, and produce a book of aerial cartoons.

There were, of course, two main problems: one was to invent a means of flying, and the second, far trickier, was to invent the humorous magazine. Not unnaturally, he managed the first far sooner: in 1783, the brothers Montgolfier rose in an aura of hot air, as one might expect from the French, and flying was born.

It took another fifty-eight years to crack the secret of the manned humorous magazine. But, at last, in 1841, Punch got off the drawing board. Even more happily, it took the drawing-board with it, which is why this book is so packed with the brilliant comedy of flight.

Which is something we'd never have had if we'd left flying strictly for the birds.

A. C.

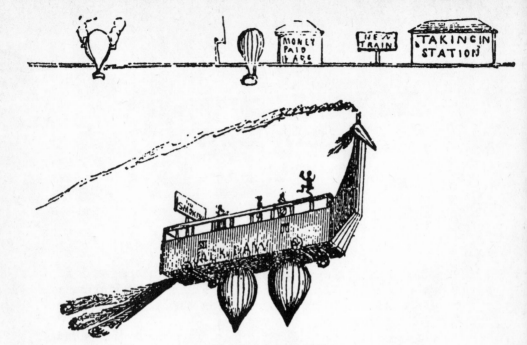

The Aerial Steam Ship

Probably by W. M. Thackeray   1843

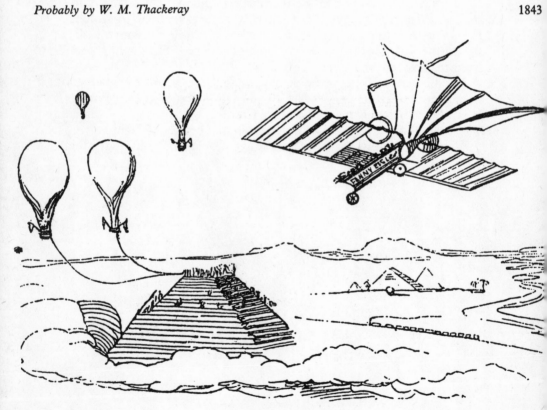

The Aerial Steam Carriage

Probably by W. M. Thackeray   1843

Early Days

GRAND INVENTION!
India in two Hours!!—Punch's Aerial Courier the Gull!!!

Probably by Richard Doyle   1843

OUT OF THEIR RECKONING

Pilot. "Where are we?"
Mechanician (who is taking fog soundings) "Piccadilly, I reckon!"

H. E. Miller

The Peaceful English Lane of the Future

Charles L. Pott

1903

"UP ABOVE THE WORLD SO HIGH"
Housebreaker. "Well, that don't look to me 'ardly safe some'ow."

Ernest Blaikley

1909

A LATE BEGINNER

Haldane (the Hawker). "I've only just taken to this sport,
but I mean to be a match for any of them."

L. Raven-Hill

1912

RIDERS OF THE WIND

John Prospero Bull. "Ariel, thy charge exactly is performed, but there's more work"

The Tempest, Act 1, Sc. 2

L. Raven-Hill

1915

The First World War

Observer. "I'm blessed if I know where we are."
Pilot. "Well, we can't be over the German lines or we should hear the
Kaiser addressing his troops."

H. E. Loughridge   1916

First Officer. "Well, where are you bound for, old chap?"
R.F.C. Officer. "German lines. Twelth of August. Must give the Bosches
some shooting, don't you know."

G. D. Armour   1916

Extract from Hun airman's report. "We dropped bombs on a British formation, causing the troops to disperse, and run about in a panic-stricken manner."

. *Jennis*

1917

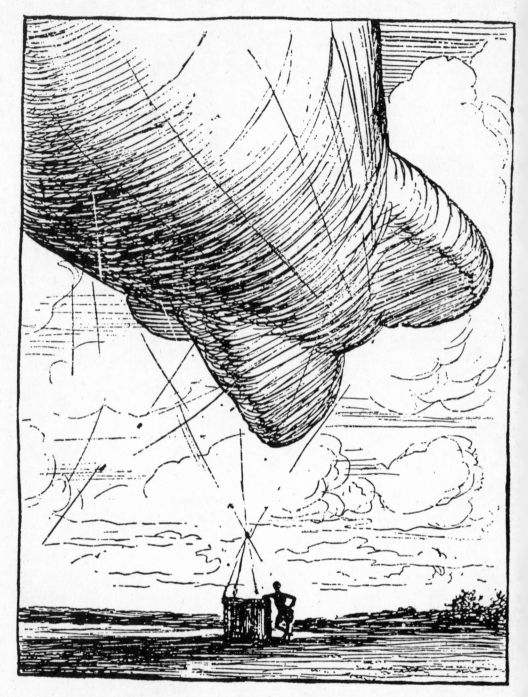

Sent in reply to following request. "Darling, do send me a picture of yourself standing by the machine you fly in."

J.H. Dowd

1918

THE NEW COMMERCIAL TRAVELLER

Puck, R.A.F. (*to Shakespeare*). "Your idea of a girdle about the earth in forty minutes is a bit tall; but you bet your immortality we shall get as near it as we can."

L. Raven-Hill   1919

THE R.A.F. AT HENDON

The "Paddock" Rails is the place to keep cool.

E. H. Shepard

1926

The Air War

John Tenniel   1890

Private T. Atkins. "Thank Gawd, Bill, we ain't got to referee this scrap."

E. H. Shepard

1925

Mr. Punch (going over the scene of the aerial attacks on London). "Congratulations! But I'm glad to see that some of the nicest buildings are still standing."

aven-Hill

Workman (*watching aeroplane*). "I don't know what you think about it, Bill, but I'd sooner be down 'ere than up there."

G. L. Stampa   1928

"And what exactly is the function of the propeller?"
"To keep the pilot cool."

J. H. Dowd   1928

Parachute Inventor (to Airman). "Now do your very best. If it doesn't open I'm ruined."

Frank R. Grey

1932

Airman. "W-what's this place?"
Convict. "Glorious Devon."

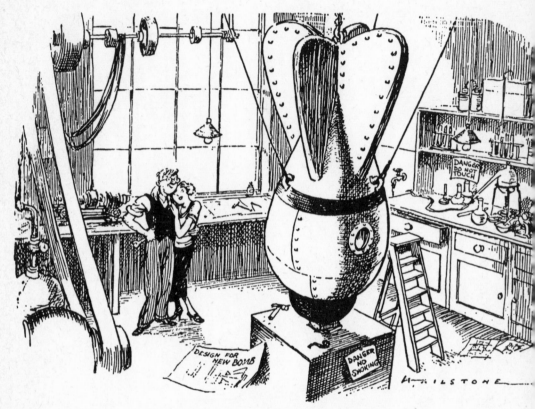

"Darling, if only the Air Ministry will accept it ... "

"It has been the fastest one of its type in the world for almost a week now."

Popular misconception (in Germany)—the R.A.F. to-day.

Between the Wars

"Nice to be in harness again."

John Melville

1940

"But you must remember that I outnumbered them by one to three."

'Pont'

"Ah! I know where I am now—there's the Town Hall."

"I WISH I could remember whether the red goes inside or outside."

Hickey

"We're just a frying-pan short on this one."

Hewitt

"... 'Borough of Grimstone' calling 'Metal-Workers' Guild' and 'Ethels of the Empire.'"

"Well, if it isn't a Curtis, I'll bet you if it isn't a Blenheim it's a Wellington."

Charles Grave

1941

"That's five bob you owe me!"

John G. Walter 1942

"... As I was saying just before we took off ..."

Brockbank 1942

"Dummy pops off and attacks the Docks at Brest—O.K. ?"

Siggs

1941

"Late again, Parkinson."

Brockbank

"Just once over with the grease-gun, Sir, and she's all ready to drive away after tea."

David Langdon   1943

"Have a word with Carter about improving his sprinting—
otherwise we'll have to ground him."

Brockbank

"I'm afraid we shall have to leave building the new wing until after the war."

"I think it's wonderful how the little ones manage to keep up with the big ones."

Sillince

"Smartly now ... Sick Para-a-a-a-de—HALT!"

David Langdon

1944

David Langdon

1944

"Right — right — left — steady — steady …"

"Right! Now we've got that little lot off, what's the trouble with your bike?"

David Langdon

194

"Start off with, say, a saturation raid on Kiel and then lead up to
the float chamber sprocket of our Bigley Carburettor."

David Langdon 1944

"Okay—come on! Left hand well down."

David Langdon

1944

"You know how I like, Nobby—just luke-warm with bags of powdered milk and a tiny bit o' saccharine."

David Langdon 1944

"Same damn trouble every time—never anyone left to give ME a shove."

David Langdon

1945

"Yes, I think that $\frac{3}{16}$ nut on the starboard outer's prop. spinner's okay now, Corp."

David Langdon

1945

"I'm not at all sure that the Labour Exchange has sent us the right sort of man for our stuff

Emett

Cedric Rogers

High Tech

David Langdon   1955

Taylor

1948

Mahood   1953

MIND THE STEP

Brockbank   1954

DANGER
LOW—FLYING
AIRCRAFT

Meigh   1956

"Your exhaust's excessively noisy!"

Norman Mansbridge

1952

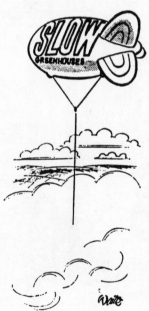

Waite   1955

"Had a little trouble losing cockpit canopies, but I think we've mastered it."

"Go easy on our plastic cucumber frames until the Service waste scare dies down."

David Langdon

1955

"Sometimes I get so fed up with our obsolete aircraft that I'd join the ruddy Navy if it wasn't for their obsolete ships."

1955

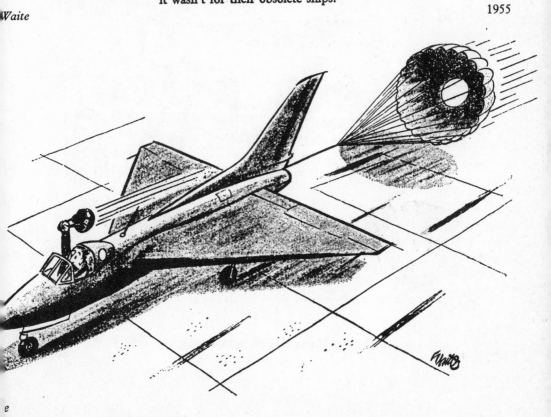

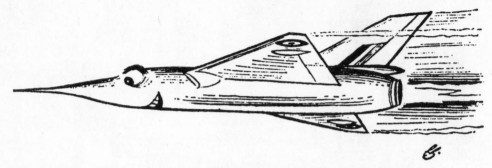

"That must be Eastbourneseafordnewhavenbrightonworthingbognor."

Brockbank   1956

"... and this is our chief test pilot."

Waite   1956

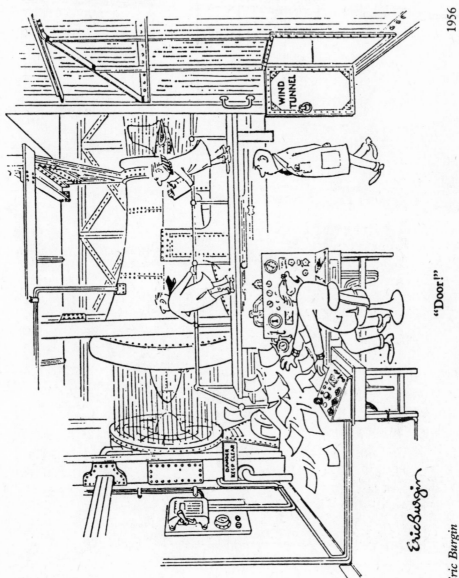

"Door!"

Eric Burgin

1956

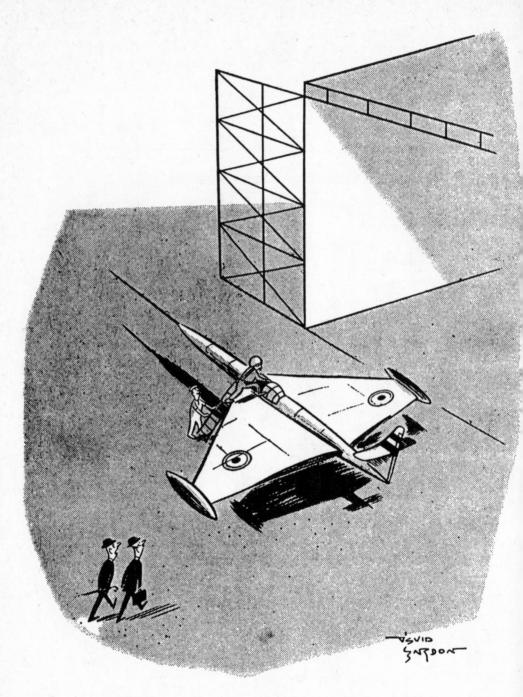

"Shall we mention it's scrapped *before* he flight-tests it?"

David Langdon

1957

" Keep 'em flying, chaps."

Tidy   1960

"Oh, dear—another one obsolete before it's off the drawing board."

Starke

1962

"Congratulations, Patton—now lick the fallout problem and we're in business."

Smilby

1962

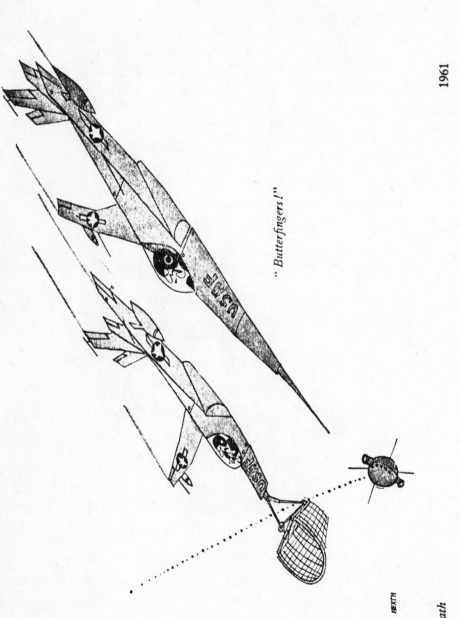

" *Butterfingers !* "

1961

Heath

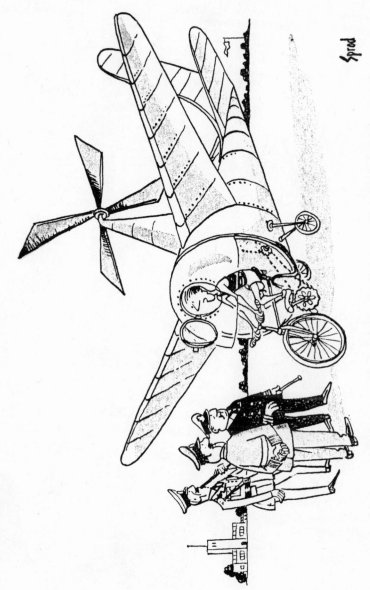

"Well, I don't know about bombs, but I might be able to carry a leaflet or two."

Sprod

1962

"*I suppose this means we'll have to cut across to the fifth.*"

"Buy Pilkington Glass, Associated Greenhouses, Allied Aspirin ..."

David Langdon   1967

HELL'S ANGELS

"If we cop it, don't let that new bombsight fall into enemy hands."

"Give 'er a couple of minutes to dry, sir."

"Oh, not another 'scramble,' sergeant."

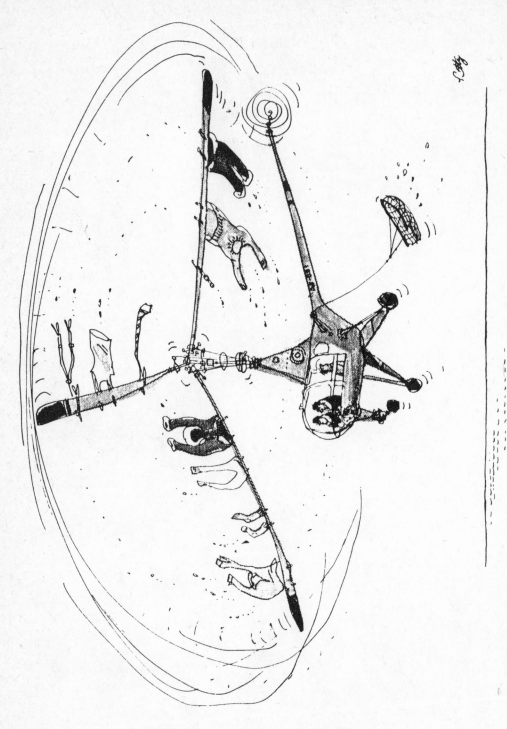

1958

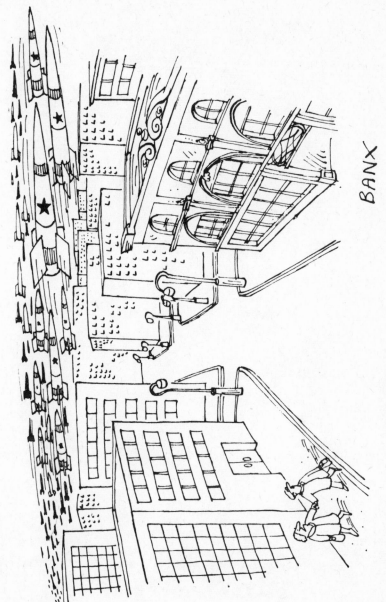

"Come on, Brian—don't let's get involved."

Banx

1981

"What's wrong with **this** chap?"

David Langdon   1968

"We've been grounded—it seems there's some design fault."

Holland   1970

The Air Fare War

David Langdon

1979

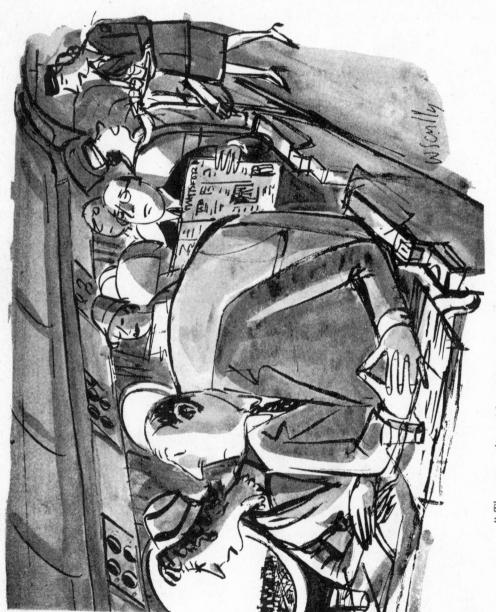

"There are plenty of parking spaces if you know where to look for them."

Scully

1962

"There they go—sipping their damned martinis."

David Langdon

1960

Bosc   1959

David Langdon 1959

"*I'm afraid there's some mistake—I'm not the hostess.*"

Scully

1960

"*I suppose she's what you have to expect on economy flights.*"

Smilby   1962

"But, m'sieurs, shouldn't we tackle the design of the aircraft first?"

ANGLO-FRENCH SUPERSONIC AIRLINER COMMITTEE

1962

David Langdon

"Good evening, ladies and gentlemen. This is your driver, Bert Higgins, welcoming you on board a London Airport Routemaster. Our estimated time of arrival at the Air Terminal is 20.30 hours, travelling, traffic permitting, at an average speed of 9 miles per hour, if that. I hope you will enjoy your journey."

David Langdon   1964

Mahood

"Damn! There goes my chance of getting through 'War and Peace' without interruption."

1966

"*You! Go back to the Economy Section!*"

Handelsman   1964

"If the worst comes to the worst, at least we travelled 'Fly now—Pay later'."

Smilby   1964

"It sounds like an uprising among the Economy Passengers. You can't blame them, the poor devils."

Handelsman

1964

"*Attention, messieurs et mesdames. C'est votre commandant. Attachez vos ceintures de sécurité et préparez-vous pour un atterrissage d'urgence.*

Achtung, meine Damen und Herren, hier spricht ihr Flugzeugführer. Bitte, befestigen sie ihren Sicherheitsgürtel und bereiten sie sich auf einer Notlandung vor.

Ladies and gentlemen, forget it. Everything is now A-OK."

Handelsman

"*Either we cut down on the free cocktails, or we forget about our passenger-safety record.*"

Smilby

1964

"We're having slight mechanical trouble but there's no need for alarm. We hope to have your picture back shortly."

Thelwell

"Oh, come now, *you* aren't tied by that frumpish, puritanical bunny-girl code!"

Starke   1966

had no idea the airlines had become so competitive."

folkes   1965

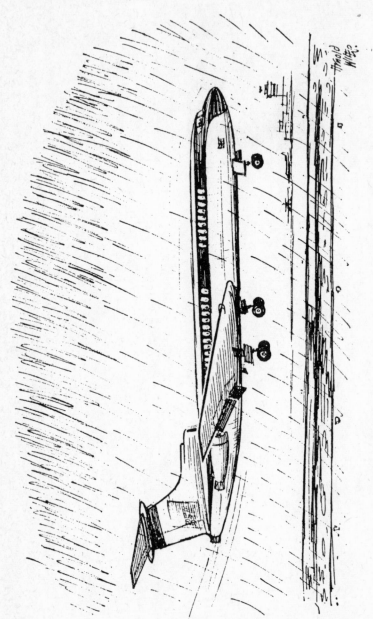

"Now comes the really dangerous part — the drive home along M4."

Wiles

1965

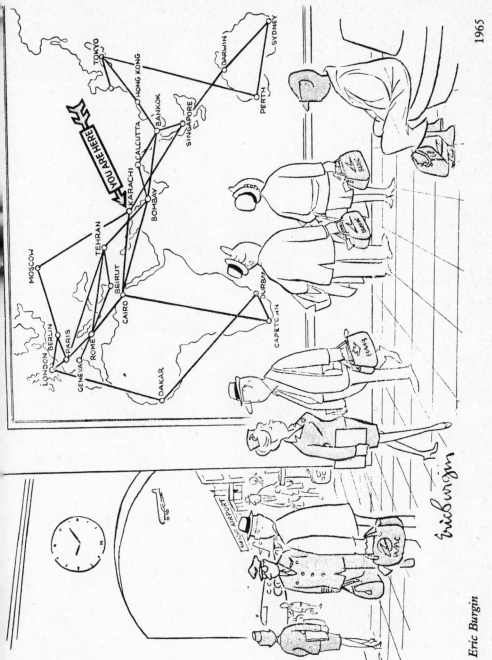

YOU ARE HERE

Eric Burgin

1965

*"Hurry up, sir—I'll **tell** you how the film ends."*

Cookson   1967

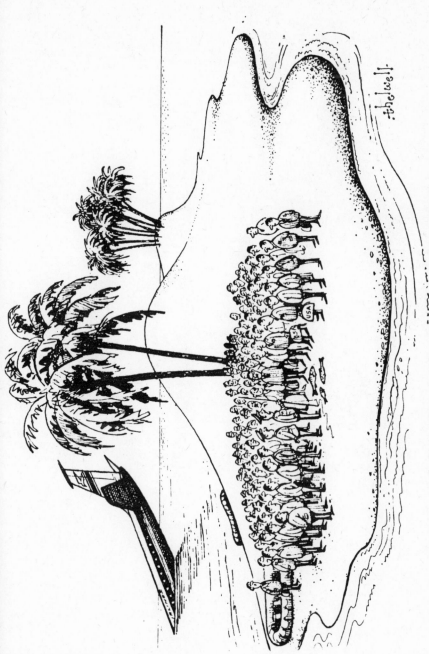

Thelwell

*"Twenty-three doctors, thirty-eight scientists and forty-one technologists.
Can't anyone cook?"*

1967

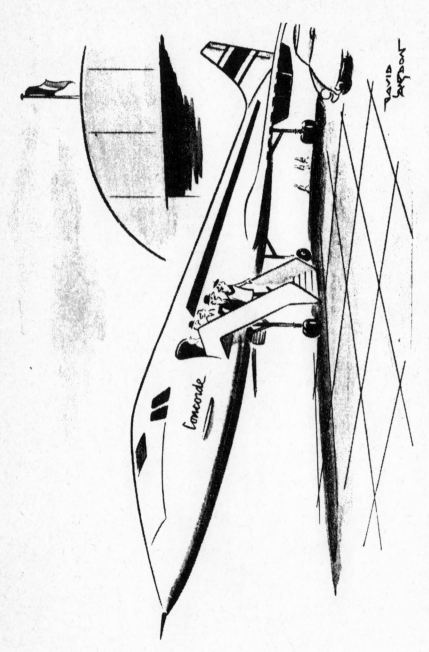

"Frankly, my Minister thought it rather tactless, the piped music 'Boom, quand notre coeur fait Boom.'"

David Langdon

"That's you and your confounded bloody cloth cap!"

Tidy

1968

"*Don't like the sound of that 'Phew!' when some of our team reach the top of the stairs.*"

David Langdon   1968

Williams   1969

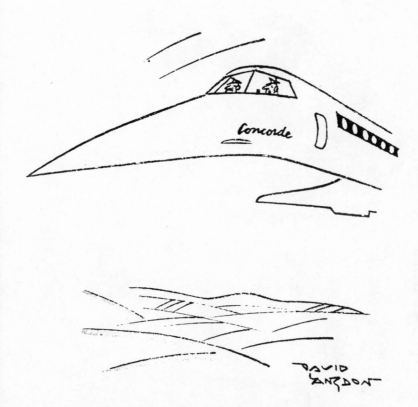

"Flight Deck to Sales Deck—where to now?"

David Langdon   1968

McLachlan

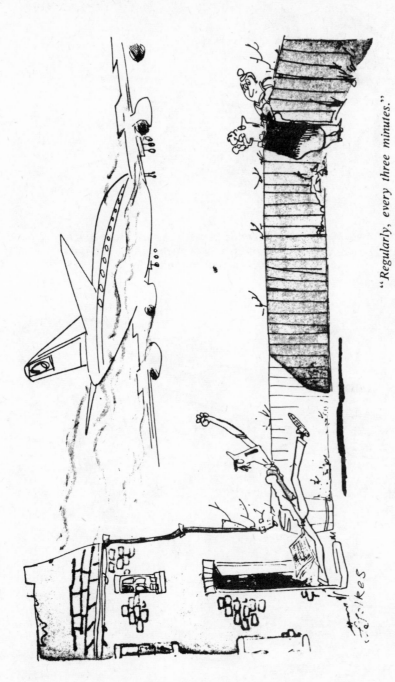

"Regularly, every three minutes."

1970

Ffolkes

"Yes, sir, I'll tell as soon as they come back from lunch. You are Captain Hawkins, you're flying a 747. and you want permission to land."

Handelsman   1973

"The standard of passenger comfort and safety leaves a lot to be desired but I must say the in-flight entertainment's a gas!"

Lowry   197

"*The trouble these days is that the jet-set is full of the people that I originally joined the jet-set to get away from!*"

Pyne   1977

COME FLY AVEC MOI

"Explain to the fool that a bidet in every toilet means losing twenty paying seats."

"Look, joint-chairman means joint-designed chairman's car—just get in and drive!"

"The perfect example of co-operation—it can fly four dozen bottles of Beaujolais Nouveau to London in twenty minutes."

"According to my diary, the date of the inaugural flight coincides with the anniversary of the Battle of Waterloo."

Dickinson

1977

"A glass of water? It's people like you
that make this route uneconomic."

"I'm afraid it's self-catering for you Discount
Fare peasants."

Dickinson

1980

*"I don't realy want to go to America—it's just that
I think Sir Freddie Laker should be supported."*

Heath   1981

*"Look, if you don't want to watch the movie you can sleep. But we
can't have you reading."*

Handelsman   1981

"All those tiny insignificant people
Particularly Mable Pendleton."

Ffolkes   1981

"It'd help us round a difficulty if you ordered a few of these rather than Harriers."

David Langdon   1981

"And I'd like to add that the hijackers were very considerate—much more than the regular crew earlier in the flight—about enforcing no-smoking regulations!"

Fisher

1981

"Any IATA ruling against my stretching out?"

David Langdon   1981

"The area we are passing over is commonly called the Bermuda Triangle."

Heath   1982

"That's the Mackenzie spread—bloody hypochondriacs."

Noel Ford

1982

"Can't get near the bloody doctor these days."

Whittock

1982

*"Ladies and gentlemen, we just crossed the International Date Line. Have **another** nice day."*

Nick   1982

"It's the annual migration to the Costa Brava!"

mikewilliams

Williams

"*Oh, good! It's the button-holes.*"

1982

*"And keep your eye on this little light at all times. If it blinks
out it means the airline has gone bankrupt."*

Fisher   1983

"Good movie. Want to hijack the plane now, or should we wait until after dinner?"

"You'll be seeing a lot of us. The kids are grown up, the dogs are dead, and we live in planes now."

*"OK, everyone's gone—you can
pick it up now."*

Nick   1982

"So sorry. Thought you'd taken early redundancy."

David Langdon   1982

"They're accurate to a thou., so there's no need to keep saying 'And the best of luck'."

Brockbank

The Space Age and Beyond

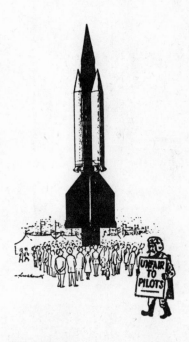

Brockbank   1957

"Same old snag—engines way ahead of airframes."

Waite   1957

"Anyway, we don't have to stand them drinks in the mess."

Brockbank

1957

"Don't *pull* the trigger—*squeeze* it."

Thelwell

Brockbank

1958

" . . . four, three, two, one, zero—Timber!"

Brockbank

"Ten—nine—eight—seven—six . . ."

Wiles   1959

Smilby

1954

Wiles   1958

"Last year it was seaweed flies."

"We'll get right to the point, senator—we're after foreign aid."

Farris

1959

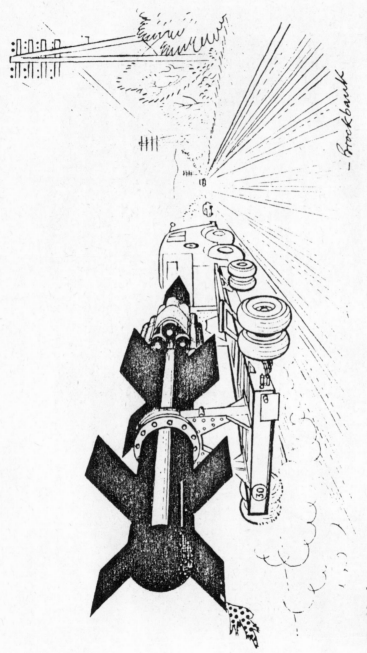

1958

Brockbank

1959

"Oh—about here, I should think."

Thelwell

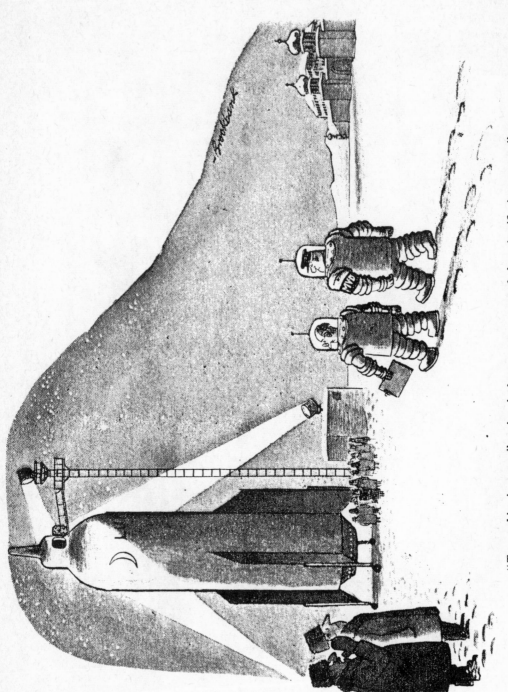

"To get him in as well we've had to remove most of the scientific instruments."

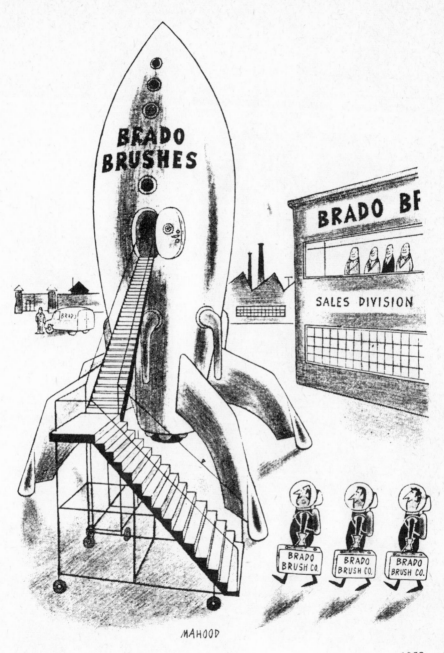

Mahood

1958

"My Government wonders whether you'd mind putting our rather expensive instrument in the recoverable part."

David Langdon   1960

"The moon's a nice place to visit, but I wouldn't want to live there."

Farris   1960

" It needs two keys to make it work, and Mum's got the other."

Heath   1960

"*Here are your rations for the trip—tomato soup, boiled beef and carrots, home—made apple pie, and the one on the end is toothpaste.*"

Sprod   1960

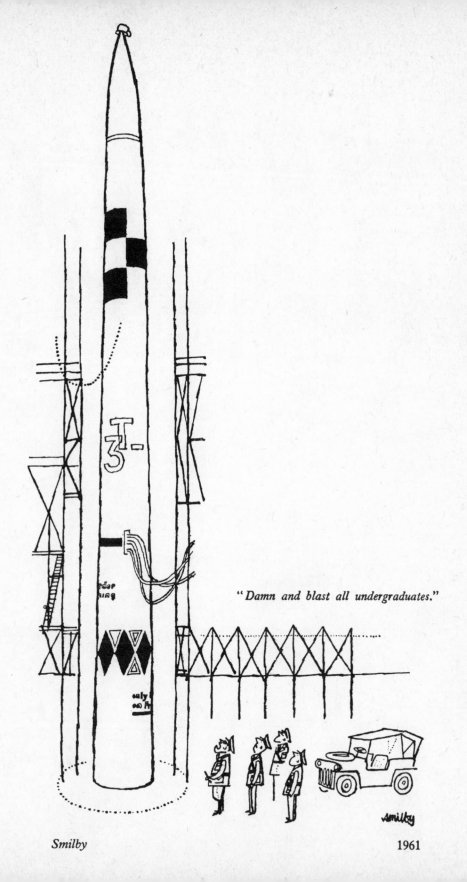

"*Damn and blast all undergraduates.*"

Smilby

1961

"But you're ALWAYS pressing the wrong button."

David Langdon

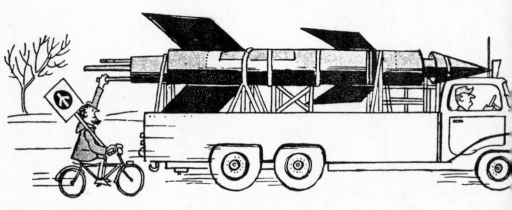

Pav

David Langdon

1962

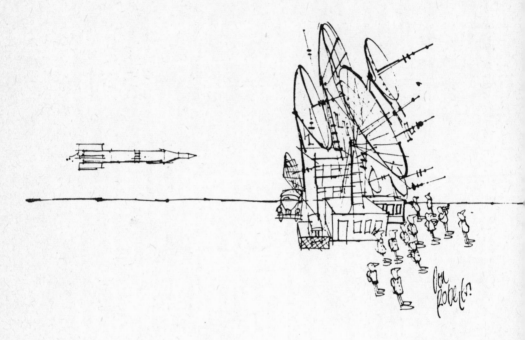

Roberts   1962

"I am Igsprx from the planet Thynog—take me to your toilet."

Williams

1983

"*I understand he's wearing a British eorn plaster.*"

Heath   1965

Starke   1966

"Shouldn't you at least be running up and down the aisle?"

Handelsman   1968

"Hello earth . . . look, I'm not quite certain how to put this . . ."

McMurtry   1967

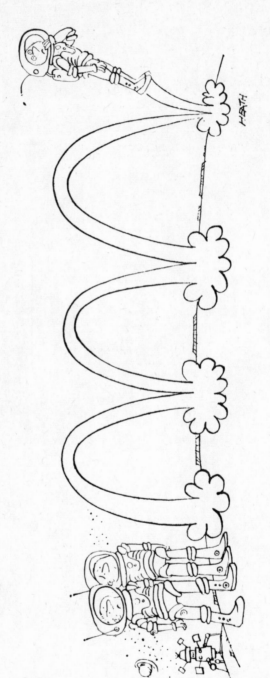

"Hiccups can be a horrible thing up here, Carter!"

Heath

1967

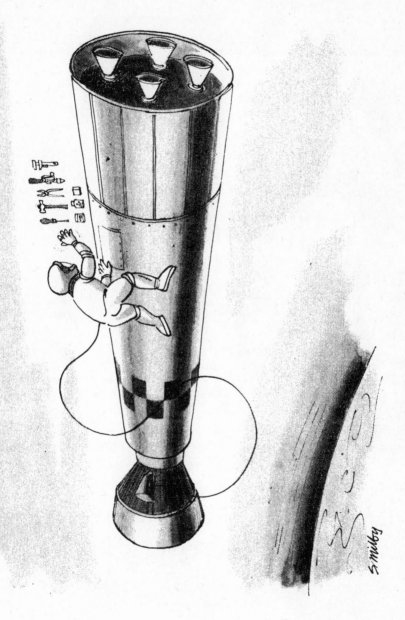

1968

Smilby

"Bit of an unscientific gesture that, after twenty-four billion dollars on research and development."

David Langdon

1973

"According to my reckoning the only aircraft scheduled to fly over this territory in the near future is Apollo 9."

Cookson   1969

"Doesn't it make you sick? Our baggage has been sent to Jupiter."

Nick   1978

*"And how much has **that** bloody thing cost the ratepayers?"*

Noel Ford   1981

"What did I tell you? See one planet and you've seen them all."

"You have a go in ours, and we'll have a go in yours, okay?"

Donegan

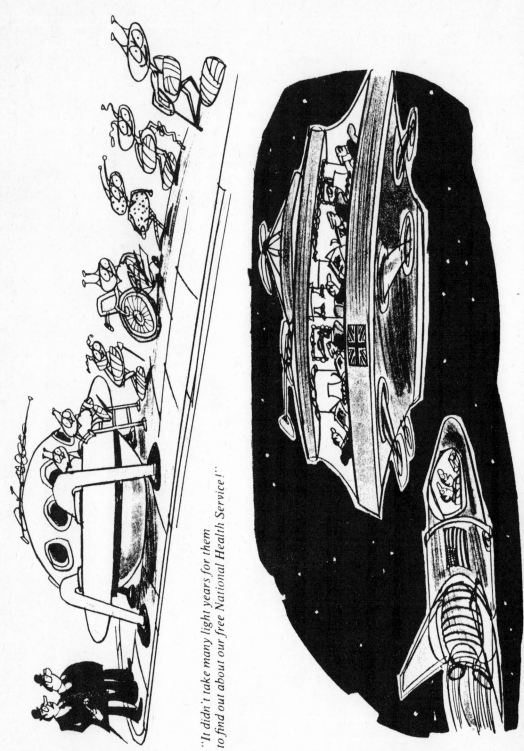

"It didn't take many light years for them
to find out about our free National Health Service!"

"The villagers must be far more sophisticated than we suspected—that's a Cruise, ground-to-air, nuclear stake through the heart!"

Lowry

1977

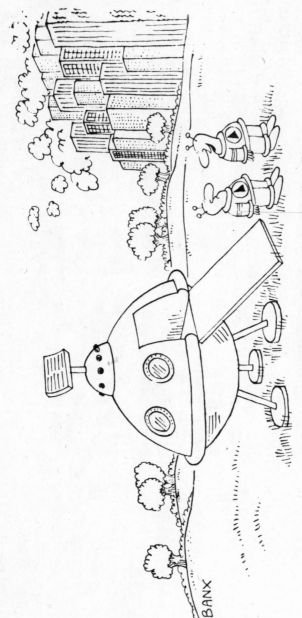

"This is the bit I like best—flouting their rabies laws."

1982

Banx

"We were rather hoping for a deep insight into trans-galactic space drive technology—we already have glass beads."

Noel Ford   1982

"For heaven's sake! No! No! No!"

Fischetti   1958

"Keep still—he's nearly got it."

Bill Stott   19

"Well, must dash, the tour itinerary gives us only 32·46 minutes for this solar system."

Noel Ford   1981

"Artie, how would you pack if you were going to Mars?"

Martin   1981

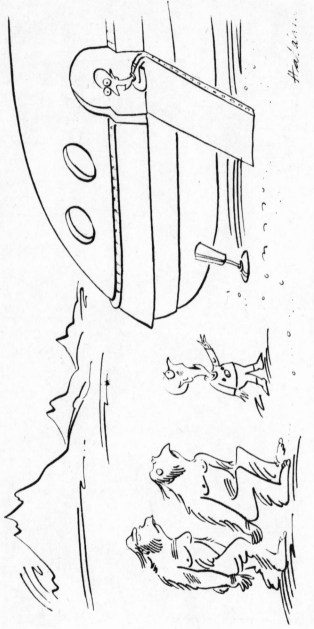

"All they want is the secret of fire, so we're stuck with 52,000,000 digital watches."

Haldane

1982

"Actually, we are from another planet, but we're not quite as advanced as you are."

Heath

1980

"It's no wonder we're an endangered species, really."

Banx   1983